Family UNplanning

A Guide for Christian Couples Seeking
God's Truth on Having Children

Craig Houghton

Foreword by Nancy Campbell
Above Rubies Magazine

This book is dedicated to my beautiful and godly helpmeet, Michelle, and the fruit of her womb: Joel, Jesse, Rachel, Naomi, Faith, Miriam, Bethany, Jared, and Jacob.

FOREWORD

""The new-born babe is a fresh act of God. He is the latest revelation of God's creative handiwork."
S. D. Gordon

Do we know what we believe? Do we know the God whom we believe? Many times, without planning, our thinking becomes the thinking of society around us. *Family UNplanning* by Craig Houghton challenges our thinking. It leads us to check whether our belief premise lines up with the Word of God or whether it is rooted in the humanistic culture in which we live.

Psalm 113 asks the question, "Who is like the Lord our God?" We would think that the proceeding verses would tell us about our mighty awesome God, the one who spread out the heavens and treads upon the waves of the sea, the one who does great things past finding out and wonders without number.

But what does the Scripture say? This psalm surprises us with the answer. It tells us that He is the one who raises the poor out of the dust and lifts the needy out of the rubbish heap! He is the one who gives the barren woman a home and makes her a joyful mother of children!

Our God aligns himself with the poor and those who have a humble spirit. He is interested in mothers and children. As we continue to search the Scriptures, we find that He is a God who loves children. The Old Testament alien gods hated children. They demanded the sacrifice of children. The same false gods are operating today through the vehicles of abortion and contraception.

Satan hates children. He comes to rob, kill and destroy. But the God of the Bible loves children. It is His greatest blessing to His created beings. After God created Adam and Eve, the first thing He did was to bless them. What was the blessing? The blessing of conception and fruitfulness-"Be fruitful, multiply and replenish the earth."

He gave them more than that. He gave them the blessing of taking dominion over the earth, but the first blessing was the blessing of children. We see the same truth in the blessing and cursing chapter of Deuteronomy 28. God pours out His blessings upon those who obey His commandments-the blessings of overflowing prosperity. But once again, we notice that this first blessing is the fruit of the womb! After that God pours out the other blessings-productive fields and fertile flocks, baskets overflowing with fruit and vegetables, kneading bowls filled with bread, storehouses filled with grain, abundance of all good things and the power to conquer enemies. All these blessings come after the blessing of the fruit of the womb. They are for the purpose of providing for the fruit of the womb.

There are many who want blessing and prosperity, but without the fruit of the womb. They want bigger houses and bigger cars, but fewer children. This doesn't line up with the Bible. Nor does it reveal the character of our God. Big houses are for many children. Big cars are for lots of children.

Our God is a God of life. He is the author of life. One of the most touching Scriptures in the Bible is in 2 Samuel 12:24 telling of the birth of Solomon. After he was born, it says, "And the LORD loved him." God loves babies. He loves giving mothers babies. He loves to see them grow into godly men and women who will reveal His image in the earth. This is His greatest blessing. He wants the world to be filled with His glory, the glory of the godly seed blessing the earth.

Frank Boreham writes, "We fancy that God can only manage His world by big battalions abroad, when all the while He is doing it by beautiful babies at home. When a wrong wants righting, or a truth wants preaching, or a continent wants opening, God sends a baby into the world to do it. That is why, long, long ago, a Babe was born in Bethlehem."

Every new babe is another image of God in this world. What a privilege to bring more of the image of God into this world.

May God bless you as you open your heart to truth and as you search the Scriptures outlined in this book.

NANCY CAMPBELL
Above Rubies magazine

Family UNplanning

A guide for Christian couples seeking
God's truth on having children

Introduction

I'm sure the first thing that comes to your mind is why this brief book is titled "Family UNplanning"? In a nutshell, I believe that today in our Western Christian culture we desperately need God's perspective on family planning. We need to encourage one another to abandon man's perspective on this entire issue and seek God's perspective, which is the only one we really require.

The question I hope to address in part is "Since when did God's children take the creation of new life into their own hands?" The Bible cautions us not to place any faith in what we think is the best course of action. We read this in Proverbs 3: 5,6;

> **5 Trust in the LORD with all thine heart; and lean not unto thine own understanding.**
> **6 In all thy ways acknowledge him, and he shall direct thy paths.**

We must ask ourselves, "Do we have the wisdom and discernment apart from God's Word to plan for the number of children that would be ideal for our family?" We need to acknowledge that our God has wonderful plans for us, and we need to let Him have full access to our lives. Jeremiah 29:11 reminds us,

[11] For I know the thoughts that I think toward you, saith the LORD, thoughts of peace, and not of evil, to give you an expected end.

And again, in Jeremiah 10: 23 the LORD tells us that He will be our Guide and that we acknowledge Him as Master of our lives.

[23]O LORD, I know that the way of man is not in himself: it is not in man that walketh to direct his steps.

We will look at the question of whether or not God is still in the business of opening and closing wombs. And of great importance is considering whether we believe that children are indeed a blessing and even a reward from our LORD as clearly laid out in Psalm 127.

[3] Lo, children are an heritage of the LORD: and the fruit of the womb is his reward.
[4] As arrows are in the hand of a mighty man; so are children of the youth.

⁵ **Happy is the man that hath his quiver full of them: they shall not be ashamed, but they shall speak with the enemies in the gate.**

I hope to challenge you to consider if the third child given to you would be as much of a blessing as the first? How about the fifth child, or even the ninth? Surely children cease to be a blessing after a certain number – or perhaps that's only what the world and the prince of the world would have us believe.

My suggestion is that we consider what many would label as a radical idea – Family UNplanning. Simply allowing our Sovereign and gracious God to be the One who plans our families.

The question really becomes, "Can we trust God to do a better job of planning our families than ourselves?" If the reasonable response of the believer is to say "Yes, the LORD's way is the best", then let us together consider family UNplanning.

TABLE OF CONTENTS

CHAPTER ONE

God's perspective on children

God loves children! Most believers have grown up with hymns too numerous to mention that attest to God's love for His little ones. "Jesus loves the little children" was one of my favorites as a youngster, and even then I believed that He really did love me.

But our source of Truth must come from God's inerrant Word, not from hymns, no matter how moving they might be. So, what does God think of children? A story recorded in Matthew, Mark, and Luke clearly demonstrates our LORD's heart for children. From Matthew 18:1-5 we read,

> [1] **At the same time came the disciples unto Jesus, saying, Who is the greatest in the kingdom of heaven?**

² And Jesus called a little child unto him, and set him in the midst of them,
³ And said, Verily I say unto you, Except ye be converted, and become as little children, ye shall not enter into the kingdom of heaven.
⁴ Whosoever therefore shall humble himself as this little child, the same is greatest in the kingdom of heaven.
⁵ And whoso shall receive one such little child in my name receiveth me.

Jesus wants ALL of us to enter the kingdom of heaven like a child. The LORD wants us to be humble of heart, like a child. How many of us have become proud because of our accomplishments, achievements, or accumulation of things? We have long since lost our innocence and become puffed-up in our self-congratulations on how we've managed. Ultimately, we know that the LORD will lift up the humble, but will bring down the proud. Note that the greatest in God's kingdom is one who possesses the same humility as a little child.

The LORD also makes it clear that when we receive a little child in His name we are receiving Him as well. Can we believe this to mean that by receiving His blessing and His reward into our families we are in essence receiving the LORD Himself? When we acknowledge a child as truly coming from the giver of all gifts, then we receive a greater knowledge of the wonders of our God.

The LORD also sternly warns anyone who would cause a child to stumble. From Mark 9:42 we receive this warning,

> **⁴² And whosoever shall offend one of these little ones that believe in me, it is better for him that a millstone were hanged about his neck, and he were cast into the sea.**

Yikes! Our LORD is obviously very serious about protecting the children who believe in Him. God loves the little children.

In order to obtain a clearer picture of what God's perspective is on children, we need to go back to the very beginning to look at why He created the institution of marriage. In Gen 2:24 we read,

> **²⁴ Therefore shall a man leave his father and his mother, and shall cleave unto his wife: *and they shall be one flesh.***

One flesh beautifully describes the union that the LORD designed for a married couple. In the process of becoming one flesh the wonders of conception occur and children are brought into the marriage relationship. We can be certain that this is the LORD's desire for the marriage bed from Malachi 2:15;

> **¹⁵ And did not he make one? Yet had he the residue of the spirit. And wherefore one? *That he might seek a godly seed.* Therefore take heed to your spirit, and let**

none deal treacherously against the wife of his youth.

The one flesh that the LORD creates is so that He might have a godly seed. God wants the marriage union to result in children. Further, Scripture tells us that the godly offspring are His. The LORD lays claim to the children of believers. We can get a glimpse of God's perspective on children in that He wants the married couple to have children while thoroughly enjoying the process of procreation. Then He claims these children as His own.

Throughout Scripture, we read of women who felt blessed if they had children, and conversely believed that they were cursed if they were barren. We need to start in Genesis 29:31 where we observe,

[31] And when the LORD saw that Leah was hated, he opened her womb: but Rachel was barren.

The LORD could see that Leah was not favored by Jacob, so the LORD comforted her by opening her womb and blessing her with children. Throughout this story, we see how God continued to bless Leah by allowing her to bear Jacob children, but at the same time Rachel remained barren and she grew increasingly desperate to bear children. In Genesis 30:22, the LORD "remembers" Rachel and blesses her with her heart's desire.

²² And God remembered Rachel, and God hearkened to her, and opened her womb.

Jacob was blessed with twelve sons as well as daughters. As Jacob neared the end of his life, he wanted to pass his blessing onto his sons who would become the twelve tribes of Israel. His blessing is found in Genesis 49, and specifically in verse 25;

²⁵ Even by the God of thy father, who shall help thee; and by the Almighty, who shall bless thee with blessings of heaven above, blessings of the deep that lieth under, blessings of the breasts, *and of the womb*:

Blessings of the womb. Jacob wanted to include in his blessing to his sons that they would be blessed, as he was, with many children. The nation of Israel was founded on Jacob and his sons. Over time, the LORD placed Israel into bondage in Egypt, but then some 400 years later delivered them through the Red Sea. Through Moses, the LORD pronounced a blessing on Israel if they were to keep His commands, but also a curse if they were to disobey. God's blessing was clear, as found in Deut 7:13;

¹³ And he will love thee, and bless thee, and multiply thee: *he will also bless the fruit of thy womb*, and the fruit of thy land, thy corn, and thy wine, and thine oil, the increase of thy kine, and the flocks of thy

sheep, in the land which he sware unto thy fathers to give thee.

The first blessing mentioned by the LORD is to multiply the nation of Israel – to bless the fruit of the womb. The list continues with blessings in many other areas as well, but first and foremost will be children. Deut 28: 4 and 11 repeat the blessing of the fruit of the womb. However, the nation of Israel was warned that disobedience would bring just the opposite. Deut 28:18 reads,

[18] Cursed shall be the fruit of thy body, and the fruit of thy land, the increase of thy kine, and the flocks of thy sheep.

God's curse would again first and foremost be a lack of children. This is God's idea of a curse! You may think that in today's climate this no longer applies, but God hasn't revealed that He has changed His way of thinking.

Does the LORD want to bless us today with children? Will it make our homes and our lives more complete if the LORD has His way in this area of our lives? The Psalmist believed it brought joy to the hearts of mothers. Psalm 113:9 states,

[9] He maketh the barren woman to keep house, and to be a joyful mother of children. Praise ye the LORD.

Yes, praise ye the LORD!

Our culture today leads us to believe that barrenness is the true blessing. Young couples are encouraged to spend time getting to know one another, establish their careers, save for the down payment on their house, pay off those students loans, etc., etc. Those same couples are told, often by fellow believers, that the last thing you need when you're just starting off is to have children. The world tells us that material stuff and self-fulfillment are the greatest need for couples. How this flies in the face of God's design for marriage. To most people, His blessing a couple with children is in reality viewed as a curse. How totally we have lost God's ideal for families and perverted our way of thinking. The saints of old desired children. The saints of today discourage children.

The LORD is with us from the beginning of life. Psalm 139:13-16 reminds us,

¹³ For thou hast possessed my reins: thou hast covered me in my mother's womb.
¹⁴ I will praise thee; for I am fearfully and wonderfully made: marvellous are thy works; and that my soul knoweth right well.
¹⁵ My substance was not hid from thee, when I was made in secret, and curiously wrought in the lowest parts of the earth.
¹⁶ Thine eyes did see my substance, yet being unperfect; and in thy book all my members were written, which in continuance were fashioned, when as yet there was none of them.

From Job 10:11,

[11] Thou hast clothed me with skin and flesh, and hast fenced me with bones and sinews.

And yet again in Jeremiah 1:5,

[5] Before I formed thee in the belly I knew thee; and before thou camest forth out of the womb I sanctified thee, and I ordained thee a prophet unto the nations.

It is the LORD who has created us, and created all humans throughout history. It never was the husband and wife who created life, for God alone is the Creator. Perhaps it is time to allow the Creator to be creative in our reproduction. Remember, Jesus loves the little children.

CHAPTER TWO

Old Testament Scriptures relating to children

We have already looked at several Old Testament Scriptures in the previous chapter to gain God's perspective on children. Let us take a closer look at God's revelation to mankind from the beginning of time, and then through His dealings with the nation of Israel. We need to start with a reminder from Hebrews 13:8 that,

> **8 Jesus Christ the same yesterday, and today, and for ever.**

The LORD who has revealed Himself in the Old Testament has not changed, and His plan from the beginning of creation has never been rescinded. He is our unchangeable LORD.

Starting in the first chapter of Genesis and following close on the heels of the creation of man and woman, God's first command to humans is found in verse 28,

> **[28] And God blessed them,** *and God said unto them, Be fruitful, and multiply*, **and replenish the earth, and subdue it: and have dominion over the fish of the sea, and over the fowl of the air, and over every living thing that moveth upon the earth.**

It is a clear instruction that man and woman were to have lots of children. It certainly isn't multiplying to have 1.5 children per couple using today's birthrate in Canada, where I reside (Wall Street Journal – January 4th, 2006). Actually, that seems to be more of being unfruitful and subtracting. In any event, God created a magnificent world and desired that mankind be obedient and fill it with people.

Soon after man sinned, all of mankind was an abomination to His eyes and He prepared to send the flood to destroy the evil upon the earth. Only Noah and his family were spared, and upon disembarking from the ark, God once again repeated His command (Genesis 9:7),

> **[7] And you,** *be ye fruitful, and multiply*; **bring forth abundantly in the earth, and multiply therein.**

God's desire remained that His people be fruitful and multiply. A new and hostile environment was apparently no reason to be cautious about having children. God didn't instruct the survivors of the flood to build homes, toil on the land, gain some material possessions, etc., but again to first and foremost fill His earth with His children.

In the previous chapter we saw how the LORD blessed both Leah and Rachel by opening their wombs and providing children. Another look at this story as found in Genesis 30:1 and 2 provides further insight;

> **¹ And when Rachel saw that she bare Jacob no children, Rachel envied her sister; and said unto Jacob, Give me children, or else I die.**
> **² And Jacob's anger was kindled against Rachel: and he said, Am I in God's stead, who hath withheld from thee the fruit of the womb?**

Firstly, we see that Rachel envied Leah because she was able to bear children but Rachel herself remained barren. With a heart of both envy and despair she pleaded with Jacob to give her children. Next, we have Jacob's response, which was to acknowledge that it was within God's sovereignty to open or close the womb as He desired. Jacob was obviously capable of impregnating his wife, but it remained within the LORD's control whether or not conception took place.

We all know of couples, whether believers or not, who think that family planning is completely within their control. Many have a master plan for their lives and have pencilled in when to have their children, how far to space them, and then when to cut off their seed. We know that seldom does this schedule work out as many have planned. But whether we meet our family goals or not, we have denied that God is still the God who opens and closes wombs at His will. Our plans are unlikely to be in step with His plans, just as Rachel's desire to have children would be fulfilled, but in God's timing.

We move on to Israel's bondage in Egypt. The Scripture paints a grim picture for the nation of Israel in slavery, and the book of Exodus tells us that life was extremely difficult and harsh. If the people of Israel ever had a good reason to want to limit the number of children they had, this was as good a time as any. Once again we see that God's ways are not our ways, and His thoughts are not our thoughts. Exodus 1:7 and 8 provides a glimpse of Israel before slavery, followed by Exodus 1: 12 and 20 when the people were under Egyptian domination.

> **⁷ And the children of Israel were fruitful, *and increased abundantly, and multiplied*, and waxed exceeding mighty; and the land was filled with them.**
> **⁸ Now there arose up a new king over Egypt, which knew not Joseph.**

Then,

> **¹² But the more they afflicted them, *the more they multiplied and grew*. And they**

were grieved because of the children of Israel.

²⁰ Therefore God dealt well with the midwives: and *the people multiplied*, and waxed very mighty.

We need to note that the LORD multiplied the people of Israel both before and after their bondage. The faithfulness of the Israelite midwives caused the LORD to continue to bless them with many children. The greater the people's affliction, the greater in number they grew.

Today we are easily deceived into putting off having children or limiting the number of our offspring due to perceived hardships. Our comfortable lifestyles have lulled us into an unreal understanding of what hardships really entail. And even then, God doesn't think that limiting children is the solution to pull us out of the problem. In fact, God's solution to the trials and tribulation of the people of Israel was to multiply them.

The growing number of Israelites gravely concerned the Egyptians. We can only assume that the Egyptians, in their prosperity, were either not being blessed numerically, or that they were practicing a form of birth control. It is well documented that both birth control and abortion were known to civilizations even at this time in history (The Columbia Electronic Encyclopedia, 6th ed., 2004). During the bondage of the people of Israel, the LORD continued to bless them in the way He knew would be well received by His people – with children.

Later on in Scripture, we are told of the great devotion of Hannah and of her plea to God to open her womb. In 1Samuel 1:8-10 we read,

> **⁸ Then said Elkanah her husband to her, Hannah, why weepest thou? and why eatest thou not? and why is thy heart grieved?** *am not I better to thee than ten sons?*
> **⁹ So Hannah rose up after they had eaten in Shiloh, and after they had drunk. Now Eli the priest sat upon a seat by a post of the temple of the LORD.**
> **¹⁰ And she was in bitterness of soul, and prayed unto the LORD, and wept sore.**

"Am not I better to thee than ten sons?" I wonder if that would catch on today as a phrase describing great blessing? The obvious impression we are left with from this Scripture is that ten sons is a standard of great blessing, not of grief and hardship. As far as Hannah was concerned, only a child could fulfill the desire of her heart.

The LORD did bless Hannah with a son, Samuel, whom she dedicated to full time service to the LORD. As a result of Hannah's faithfulness in her giving of Samuel to Eli the priest, we read of her reward from God in 1Samuel 2:21.

21 And the LORD visited Hannah, so that she conceived, and bare three sons and two daughters. And the child Samuel grew before the LORD.

What was Hannah's reward for her service to God? Five more children! Certainly it is clear that the LORD's idea of a reward is to open the womb of the woman and to bless the family with children. God's blessing on His people is shown in much the same manner from the Scripture that provides us with the lineage of little-known Obededom, whom the LORD provided eight sons. From 1Chronicles 26: 4-5;

4 Moreover the sons of Obededom were, Shemaiah the firstborn, Jehozabad the second, Joah the third, and Sacar the fourth, and Nethaneel the fifth.
5 Ammiel the sixth, Issachar the seventh, Peulthai the eighth: *for God blessed him.*

Once our LORD blesses us with children, He not only commands us, but also gives us the privilege of training our children to know and to love Him. God's plan involves the parents raising up the next generation of believers for His glory. We read these instructions in Deut 6:6-9;

6 And these words, which I command thee this day, shall be in thine heart:
7 And thou shalt teach them diligently unto thy children, and shalt talk of them

> **when thou sittest in thine house, and when thou walkest by the way, and when thou liest down, and when thou risest up.**
> **⁸ And thou shalt bind them for a sign upon thine hand, and they shall be as frontlets between thine eyes.**
> **⁹ And thou shalt write them upon the posts of thy house, and on thy gates.**

These commandments may seem overwhelming, but once again we are reminded that in the flesh we are destined to fail, but with the help and guidance of the Holy Spirit great things can be accomplished. God loves us and our children, and is in our corner to help us fulfill His plan for families.

The Old Testament also speaks generally to any nation's desire to have many people and many children. From Proverbs 14:28;

> **²⁸ In the multitude of people is the king's honour: but in the want of people is the destruction of the prince.**

In order for a king to pass along a thriving kingdom to his son, there needs to be a growing population, otherwise destruction looms on the horizon. How different the thinking of nations today that want to "stabilize" the population of their people, or ultimately see the population decrease. China is a modern day example of the short-sightedness of such a strategy. Not only has it led to rampant infanticide and abortion, it has created a culture where at present there are 120 boys registered as born for every 100 girls babies (BBC News, World Edition, 06January2004). The Western World has no such official one-child policy, but the philosophy remains the same that the fewer people there are, the more there will be for the rest of us. A brief glimpse to the future of our Old Age Security programs will confirm that without the next generation contributing to these pensions, the money is soon to run out. In fact, instead of there being more available to those remaining, there will actually be less (The New York Times, 31December2004).

One of the arguments I often hear concerning Scriptural teachings concerning being fruitful and multiplying, is that the people of the Old Testament lived in an agrarian society and many children were needed to work the land, take care of the flocks, etc. However, I haven't found this "requirement" in Scripture that you need to be a farmer to have a large family. In fact, we read in Deut 28:34;

³ Blessed shalt thou be in the city, and blessed shalt thou be in the field.
⁴ *Blessed shall be the fruit of thy body*, and the fruit of thy ground, and the fruit of thy cattle, the increase of thy kine, and the flocks of thy sheep.

The LORD clearly indicates in this chapter of blessing to an obedient nation that He will bless them both in the city and in the field. The fruit of the body in the LORD's eyes are not limited by physical surroundings, but is limited only by our unwillingness to surrender completely to His ways. We often use the reasoning that because of our small home (or even apartment), we need to limit the fruit of the body. We need to re-evaluate whether the LORD has told us this, or if it is only worldly wisdom that causes us to think in this way.

If God chose to bless Israel with children both in the city and in the field, how would God withhold His blessing if the nation was disobedient? Deut 28: 16 to 18,

> [16] **Cursed shalt thou be in the city, and cursed shalt thou be in the field.**
> [17] **Cursed shall be thy basket and thy store.**
> [18] *Cursed shall be the fruit of thy body*, **and the fruit of thy land, the increase of thy kine, and the flocks of thy sheep.**

Cursed would be the fruit of the body. God's curse was barrenness. Do we believe that today? Or have we exalted the two-income couple who have limited the fruit of the womb as the model for both the believer and non-believer? What God calls a curse, is a curse, no matter what spin we put on it.

Finally, I need to briefly address the Scripture concerning Onan that we find in Genesis 38. There are several different views on what exactly Onan did that caused the LORD to strike him dead, but I think in light of the many Bible references we have looked at, it may have been because of his unwillingness to procreate. There was a custom of the time that if the eldest brother died without children, the nearest unmarried relative living in the household would be obliged to marry the eldest brother's wife to carry on the name of the eldest brother. This is why Judah tells Onan to marry Tamar. Interestingly, this custom later became part of the Mosaic Law that is recorded in Deut 25: 5-10:

> "If brothers are living together and one of them dies without a son, his widow must not marry outside the family. Her husband's brother shall take her and marry her and fulfil the duty of a brother-in-law to her. The first son she bears shall carry on the name of the dead brother so that his name will not be blotted out from Israel. However, if a man does not want to marry his brother's wife, she shall go to the elders at the town gate and say, `My husband's brother refuses to carry on his brother's name in Israel. He will not fulfil the duty of a brother-in-law to me.' Then the elders of his town shall summon him and talk to him. If he persists in saying, `I do not want to marry her,' his brother's widow shall go up to him in the presence of the elders, take off one of his sandals, spit in his face and say, `This is what is done to the man who will not build up his brother's family line.' That man's line shall be known in Israel

as The Family of the Unsandalled" (Deut.
25:5-10).

So we see that it was not mandatory that the next
of kin marry the eldest brother's wife, but it was
shameful for him not to marry her. Now, Judah's son
Onan agreed to marry Tamar; however, he deliberately did not fulfill his duty to produce a child for his
deceased brother:

Genesis 38
**⁸ And Judah said unto Onan, Go in unto
thy brother's wife, and marry her, and
raise up seed to thy brother.**
**⁹ And Onan knew that the seed should not
be his; and it came to pass, when he went
in unto his brother's wife, that he spilled it
on the ground, lest that he should give seed
to his brother.**
**¹⁰ And the thing, which he did, *displeased
the LORD: wherefore he slew him also.***

The LORD may have judged Onan because,
although he was willing to derive the sexual plea-
sures of being with Tamar, he prevented conception from taking place. "The thing which he did
displeased the LORD: wherefore He slew him also,"
may very well be Onan's use of what we refer to as
"coitus interruptus." This story is an illustration of
circumventing God's design of pleasure and procreation working together. Man, in his sinful state, has
separated what God intended to be part of the same

act of intimacy. Children should not be the unwanted part of the sexual union of husband and wife, but are to be greatly desired. I am not suggesting that the narrative concerning Onan teaches that sexual intimacy between a couple is *only* for procreation, but we need to re-establish the idea that pleasure and conception are not mutually exclusive in God's great plan. Just as it is a perversion of Scripture to teach that the marriage bed is strictly for conceiving children, it is also a perversion of God's Word to teach that men and women were created simply to satisfy the desires of the flesh.

The God of the Old Testament is the Sovereign One who desires to bless His people today in the same fashion that He blessed all of His Creation "in the beginning". His beautiful and wondrous design for man is revealed clearly in His Word, and His greatest blessing to His people remains the fruit of the womb.

CHAPTER THREE

New Testament Scriptures relating to children

Many who may disagree with the concept of family UNplanning will admit, reluctantly or otherwise, that the Old Testament clearly speaks of the sovereignty of conception belonging with the LORD. However, many wish to make a distinction when it comes to the New Testament and deny that the Church can rightly be compared with the Old Testament nation of Israel.

What are the New Testament Scriptures and principles that would point us to further confirmation of God's desire to be sovereign in our families and with our reproduction? Does God have a Plan A for the nation of Israel, and a Plan B for the believers in this area?

Look again at Hebrews 13:8 and what the LORD has to say about Himself.

⁸ Jesus Christ the same yesterday, and today, and for ever.

We need to seriously consider that the God who blessed the people of Israel by opening their wombs is the same God who desires to bless His people (believers) with children today.

We have already explored some of the Scriptures that reveal the LORD's tenderness toward children in a previous chapter. Jesus loves the children! His heart for them is clearly shown in these further Scriptures:

Matthew 19
¹³ Then were there brought unto him little children, that he should put his hands on them, and pray: and the disciples rebuked them.
¹⁴ But Jesus said, Suffer little children, and forbid them not, to come unto me: for of such is the kingdom of heaven.
¹⁵ And he laid his hands on them, and departed thence.

Mark 10
¹⁴ But when Jesus saw it, he was much displeased, and said unto them, Suffer the little children to come unto me, and forbid them not: for of such is the kingdom of God.

Matthew 18

[2] And Jesus called a little child unto him, and set him in the midst of them,

[3] And said, Verily I say unto you, Except ye be converted, and become as little children ye shall not enter into the kingdom of heaven.

Mark 5

[41] And he took the damsel by the hand, and said unto her, Talitha cumi; which is, being interpreted, Damsel, I say unto thee, arise.

The LORD's desire to bless and heal the children is throughout the gospels, but the next question we need to ask is if there are principles from New Testament Scripture that would encourage us to allow God to be sovereign in our family planning? Let us look at several passages that confirm this idea.

Romans 12

[1] I beseech you therefore, brethren, by the mercies of God, that ye present your bodies a living sacrifice, holy, acceptable unto God, which is your reasonable service.

[2] And be not conformed to this world: but be ye transformed by the renewing of your mind, that ye may prove what is that good, and acceptable, and perfect, will of God.

What does it mean to present our bodies as a living sacrifice? I would suggest that as a sacrifice, we have nothing further to say in regard to what the LORD does with us. How can we reason that we could be a living sacrifice, and yet still maintain control of some part of ourselves, including our reproduction? Does a sacrifice have the ability to leave part of itself off of the altar? Does it not sound somewhat hollow to come before our God and say "Here I am LORD... take most of me and use me as You see fit?" This Scripture suggests quite rightly that offering ourselves as a living sacrifice to God is our "reasonable service," and does not only apply to the heroes of our faith.

We are told to not be conformed to this world. Western Christianity has done just that. We have conformed to the culture around us and have adopted the world's thinking on families. Our admonishment from the Word is to be separate from the world. A life of separateness from the ungodly will be what attracts those to the light that we reflect from God. The more we are like the world, the less difference the unbeliever can see, and ultimately the less light we reflect as we become tarnished through conformity.

Furthermore, the Holy Spirit in this Scripture tells us to be transformed by the renewing of our mind. This one small portion of Scripture sums up the desperate need we have in our churches today. Our minds are in need of more than just some fine-tuning, but rather a complete overhaul. In fact, we need a transformation from one way of thinking (worldly) to a totally different way of looking at things (Biblical). This Scripture further reveals to us that this transformation is something we need to do – a conscious decision on our part to stop thinking like the world around us, and start thinking the way God would want us to. The Holy Spirit is ever our Counsellor, and He will accomplish this transformation when we allow Him access to our thoughts and imaginations. He can transform our thinking with regard to the entire issue of having children.

Lastly, the Scripture proclaims that through the offer of ourselves as a living sacrifice, not being conformed to the world, and the transformation of our minds, that only then can we clearly discern what is "the perfect will of God." How can we really expect to know His will for us if we think, and act, like the godless world around us? We can be certain that the LORD desires to make His will known to us. He is not the mysterious and distant God that many pretend He is. He has already revealed Himself fully through Jesus Christ, and has left us His perfect Word.

Many people have asked the question, "How can I know God's will?" The answer is that for the believer, God's will has been preserved for us in His written Word, and then confirmed in our hearts through the Holy Spirit. That is what I hope to achieve through this book; a desire for each of us to read the Bible and find out what our LORD has already spoken on this matter of reproduction. Our problem is that too often we try to figure out what God's position is on a matter based on our understanding of the character of God, when we overlook that He has already spoken on the issue in clear terms.

Another New Testament Scripture that should be examined is found in 1Corinthians 6:20;

²⁰ For ye are bought with a price: there-fore glorify God in your body, and in your spirit, which are God's.

and again in 1Corinthians 7:23,

²³ Ye are bought with a price; be not ye the servants of men.

Simply, as believers we don't belong to ourselves. God is declaring that He owns us, and as owner He has full control. The price He paid for us was His Son dying on the cross and taking our sins upon Himself. It was a price beyond comprehension, and yet God's just pronouncement that the wages of sin is death could only be fulfilled by the sinless One dying the death we deserved. So, having purchased us with the precious blood of Jesus, we must ask ourselves if we still retain any part of our bodies – even our reproduction?

The purchase that God made is intended to bring glory to Him. In both our body and our spirit, we are to glorify the LORD. Since we know that God desires a godly offspring from His people, would we not accomplish giving God the glory by letting Him bless the fruit of our womb and raising these children to sing His praises?

We are also told not to be the servants of men, but of God. Do we serve God by conforming to the world, or rather by being a bondservant to Him who was the servant to all mankind? If we are His, through His purchase of us, shouldn't we willingly admit His ownership of any area of our lives to which He wants access? He owns all of us, or in reality He owns none of us.

Romans 6:11 and Ephesians 2:1, 5 provide the next area where the Bible has shown us how we are to view ourselves once we are saved through Christ.

Romans 6
¹¹ Likewise *reckon ye also yourselves to be dead* indeed unto sin, but alive unto God through Jesus Christ our Lord.

Ephesians 2
¹ And you hath he quickened, *who were dead* in trespasses and sins;
⁵ Even when we were dead in sins, hath quickened us together with Christ, (by grace ye are saved;)

Being considered dead in God's sight, we have to question what, if any, decision- making we may entertain apart from guidance by the Holy Spirit. A dead person can hardly be expected to make any decisions, especially wise ones. But the Scripture continues that not only are we dead unto ourselves, but we are alive in Christ. He is to be our source of life, and as we learn to reckon ourselves dead, He can live more fully through us. Applying these Scriptures to the issue of family planning, it would seem logical that we, being dead in our sins, are incapable of making the wise choice. However, then being considered alive in Christ, He can make the decision for us. I would suggest He has done just that in His Word, and that His choice is life: fruitful and multiplying life.

A Biblical passage that a pastor once used to defend his belief for sterilization was from 1Corinthians 7:3-5;

> **[3] Let the husband render unto the wife due benevolence: and likewise also the wife unto the husband.**
> **[4] The wife hath not power of her own body, but the husband: and likewise also the husband hath not power of his own body, but the wife.**
> **[5] Defraud ye not one the other, except it be with consent for a time, that ye may give yourselves to fasting and prayer; and come together again, that Satan tempt you not for your incontinency.**

This Scripture speaks of refraining from intimacy for a mutually agreeable timeframe, with the intention of devoting that time for prayer and fasting. It is a perversion of Scripture to suggest that this passage is condoning a permanent cutting off of our reproduction. Nor can these verses be massaged into place to support the idea of natural family planning. The abstinence period is not for refraining from sexual intercourse during the peak fertilization time, but rather only for prayer and fasting. God intends for the married couple to belong to one another, one-flesh, and this means being available for each other for friendship and intimacy.

The idea of denying ourselves to our spouses for a short period of time during the woman's ovulation has spawned what many today call Natural Family Planning (NFP). As we discussed in the previous chapter, Onan practiced a form of NFP to ensure his seed would not enter Tamar to prevent conception from taking place. Today we have natural family planning down to a science with machines and devices to calculate temperatures and cycles, usually to make sure that we avoid intimacy during the "dangerous" days. NFP is hardly natural if we use it to circumvent the reproductive system that the LORD has put into place. The most natural thing to do would be to let Nature take its course, and once again allow God to be sovereign in this area of our lives. The story of Onan from Genesis 38 is the Bible's *only* allusion to what we refer to today as NFP. This act brought the LORD's judgement, not His blessing.

Another New Testament principle that has been used by many to suggest that we should limit our offspring comes from the gospel story of the talents as found in Matthew.

Matthew 25
[15] And unto one he gave five talents, to another two, and to another one; to every man according to his several ability; and straightway took his journey.

Many will want to claim that some people are more talented than others to raise up a large family, and that some should have just one or two children. The issue however is one of stewardship and being faithful with what the Master gives to us. Once again we note that the decision of how many talents each servant received was the Master's. It was not the servant who requested one, two, or five talents, but the LORD who chose to entrust to each servant as He saw fit. With family planning in mind, we are reminded that we are to be faithful with what the LORD Himself decides to bless us with, and that we have been entrusted with these precious lives to nurture, and then instruct in the ways of righteousness.

The New Testament, in many ways, expands on the ideas put forth in the Old Testament. In the Old Testament Scriptures we find that the LORD desired to bless His people with children, and claimed sovereignty over the womb. In the New Testament we discover that not only does God want control of the womb but desires complete ownership of our entire bodies. His desire is to use us, try us, control us, and bless us at His good pleasure. It naturally follows that in order for God to use us, whom He purchased with the blood of Jesus, we can withhold nothing from Him. The God who opened and closed the wombs of His people of old is the same God who is calling us to obedience to Him this day.

1 Timothy 5
[14] **I will therefore that the younger women marry,** *bear children*, **guide the house, give none occasion to the adversary to speak reproachfully.**

CHAPTER FOUR

The first 1900 years
of the church

Evangelical Christians often use the argument that birth control (or the lack thereof) is a strictly Roman Catholic tradition, without exploring either what the Bible has to say about the issue, or discovering the traditional Protestant position on family planning.

Roman Catholics often express that the idea of not using birth control is an antiquated value of the church and that adherents are not expected to follow that teaching today. After all, isn't overpopulation already a world problem? This idea is a myth, which both believers and non-believers have shown to be an outright lie, but that discussion is better left for another time. If readers want to know more on this issue, I would suggest a read of "A Full Quiver" by Rick and Jan Hess.

In 1968, Pope Paul VI issued a letter entitled *Humanae Vitae* (Latin, "Human Life"), which reaffirmed the Catholic church teaching that it is wrong to use contraception to prevent new human beings from coming into existence.

Contraception is defined in this letter as "any action which, either in anticipation of the conjugal act [sexual intercourse], or in its accomplishment, or in the development of its natural consequences, proposes, whether as an end or as a means, to render procreation impossible" (*Humanae Vitae* 14). This includes sterilization, condoms and other barrier methods, spermicides, *coitus interruptus* (withdrawal method), the Pill, and all other such methods.

What is often unknown, especially to the Protestant, is that up until 1930, *all* Protestant denominations agreed with the Catholic Church's teaching condemning contraception as sinful. At its 1930 Lambeth Conference, the Anglican church, persuaded by a changing and less God-fearing culture, announced that contraception would be allowed in *some* circumstances. This opened the door to allowing birth control with the support of the church, and would soon lead to most churches' endorsement without conditions.

Well before the advent of Protestantism, and prior to the establishment of the Roman Catholic Church, those we have identified as the early church fathers taught that birth control was wrong. In A.D. 195, Clement of Alexandria wrote, "Because of its divine institution for the propagation of man, the seed is not to be vainly ejaculated, nor is it to be damaged, nor is it to be wasted" (*The Instructor of Children* 2:10:91:2).

Hippolytus of Rome wrote in 255 A.D. that "on account of their prominent ancestry and great property, the so-called faithful [certain Christian women who had affairs with male servants] want no children from slaves or lowborn commoners, [so] they use drugs of sterility or bind themselves tightly in order to expel a fetus which has already been engendered" (*Refutation of All Heresies* 9:12).

Around 307, Lactantius stated that some "complain of the scantiness of their means, and allege that they have not enough for bringing up more children, as though, in truth, their means were in [their] power . . . or God did not daily make the rich poor and the poor rich. Wherefore, if any one on any account of poverty shall be unable to bring up children, it is better to abstain from relations with his wife" (*Divine Institutes* 6:20).

The First Council of Nicaea in 325 stated, "If anyone in sound health has castrated himself, it behooves that such a one, if enrolled among the clergy, should cease [from his ministry], and that from henceforth no such person should be promoted. But, as it is evident that this is said of those who willfully do the thing and presume to castrate themselves, so if any have been made eunuchs by barbarians, or by their masters, and should otherwise be found worthy, such men this canon admits to the clergy" (Canon 1).

Augustine wrote in 419, "I am supposing, then, although you are not lying [with your wife] for the sake of procreating offspring, you are not for the sake of lust obstructing their procreation by an evil prayer or an evil deed. Those who do this, although they are called husband and wife, are not; nor do they retain any reality of marriage, but with a respectable name cover a shame. Sometimes this lustful cruelty, or cruel lust, comes to this, that they even procure poisons of sterility [oral contraceptives]" (*Marriage and Concupiscence* 1:15:17).

Protestant Reformers whose cries were for "Sola Scriptura" taught and believed that Scripture was clear on this matter as well. Martin Luther said, "[T]he exceedingly foul deed of Onan, the basest of wretches . . . is a most disgraceful sin. It is far more atrocious than incest and adultery. We call it unchastity, yes, a sodomitic sin. For Onan goes in to her; that is, he lies with her and copulates, and when it comes to the point of insemination, spills the semen, lest the woman conceive. Surely at such a time the order of nature established by God in procreation should be followed. Accordingly, it was a most disgraceful crime. . . . Consequently, he deserved to be killed by God. He committed an evil deed. Therefore, God punished him."

John Calvin said, "The voluntary spilling of semen outside of intercourse between man and woman is a monstrous thing. Deliberately to withdraw from coitus in order that semen may fall on the ground is doubly monstrous. For this is to extinguish the hope of the race and to kill before he is born the hoped-for offspring."

John Wesley warned, "Those sins that dishonor the body are very displeasing to God, and the evidence of vile affections. Observe, the thing which he [Onan] did displeased the Lord—and it is to be feared; thousands, especially of single persons, by this very thing, still displease the Lord, and destroy their own souls." (These passages are quoted in Charles D. Provan, *The Bible and Birth Control*, which contains many quotes by historic Protestant figures who recognized contraception's evils.)

The Catholic Church has been consistent in this matter of birth control and adherents to this church are mistaken if they believe the teaching has changed. This was reiterated in the *Catechism of the Catholic Church*: "[E]very action which, whether in anticipation of the conjugal act, or in its accomplishment, or in the development of its natural consequences, proposes, whether as an end or as a means, to render procreation impossible is intrinsically evil" (CCC 2370). "Legitimate intentions on the part of the spouses do not justify recourse to morally unacceptable means . . . for example, direct sterilization or contraception" (CCC 2399).

C.H. Spurgeon wrote a commentary on Psalm 127 in the late 1800's that espoused the Protestant view for the turn of that century. The following are a few excerpts from his Treasury of David, Psalms 127:5.

<u>Ver. 5. Happy is the man that hath his quiver full of them.</u> Those who have no children bewail the fact; those who have few children see them soon gone, and the house is silent, and their life has lost a charm; those who have many gracious children are upon the whole

the happiest. Of course a large number of children means a large number of trials; but when these are met by faith in the Lord it also means a mass of love, and a multitude of joys. The writer of this comment gives it as his own observation, that he has seen the most frequent unhappiness in marriages which are unfruitful; that he has himself been most grateful for two of the best of sons; but as they have both grown up, and he has no child at home, he has without a tinge of murmuring, or even wishing that he were otherwise circumstanced, felt that it might have been a blessing to have had a more numerous family: he therefore heartily agrees with the Psalmist's verdict herein expressed. He has known a family in which there were some twelve daughters and three sons, and he never expects to witness upon earth greater domestic felicity than fell to the lot of their parents, who rejoiced in all their children, as the children also rejoiced in their parents and in one another. When sons and daughters are arrows, it is well to have a quiver full of them; but if they are only sticks, knotty and useless, the fewer of them the better. While those are blessed whose quiver is full, there is no reason to doubt that many are blessed who have no quiver at all; for a quiet life may not need such a warlike weapon. Moreover, a quiver may be small and yet full; and then the blessing is obtained. In any case we may be sure that a man's life consisteth not in the abundance of children that he possesseth....

"Thy seed shall possess the gate of his enemies"; and it is sure to all the beloved of the Lord in some sense or other. Doth not the Lord Jesus thus triumph in his seed? Looked at literally, this favour cometh of the Lord: without his will there would be no children to build up the house, and without his grace there would be no good children to be their parent's strength. If this must be left with the Lord, let us leave every other thing in the same hands. He will undertake for us and prosper our trustful endeavours, and we shall enjoy a tranquil life, and prove ourselves to be our Lord's beloved by the calm and quiet of our spirit. We need not doubt that if God gives us children as a reward he will also send us the food and raiment which he knows they need....

I would not even dare to try to add to the eloquence of Charles Spurgeon, nor any of the early church fathers. The point I hope to make in this chapter is that the current Protestant view of birth control that we know of today was an idea unknown and unsupported by the church for its first 1900 years of existence. Not that there weren't dissenting voices from other church leaders during this time, but by far the church understood that God had clearly spoken on this entire matter in Scripture and His sovereignty was not to be challenged.

I end this chapter with a quote from a 17th century poet and statesman that makes my heart rejoice in its beauty.

I remember a great man coming into my house, at Waltham, and seeing all my children standing in the order of their age and stature, said, "These are they that make rich men poor." But he straight received this answer, "Nay, my lord, these are they that make a poor man rich; for there is not one of these whom we would part with for all your wealth." *Joseph Hall, 1574-1656*

CHAPTER FIVE

How did we get to where we are today?

How did our Western Christianity get to the point where it is at today with regard to family planning? The bold, new idea that men and women could and should control their reproduction is here, but how did it arrive? It certainly didn't appear overnight, or faithful Christians who were on guard would have sounded the alarm. It didn't enter into our churches by storming the front doors and holding us captive, otherwise we would have recognized it quickly and clearly as a deception from Satan meant to destroy us. But came it did, and not only did the church not protest its intrusion, we have since embraced it, taught it, promoted it, and preached it.

There are many events and people, philosophies and circumstances that have shaped our culture's thinking over the past 100 years resulting in a society more independent of God and more dependent on ourselves. This past century has seen two major world wars and localized wars too numerous to count. Materialism has gripped the hearts of most in the Western world, and "things" and "stuff" have replaced relationships.

One of the major philosophies that shapes our culture is the theory of evolution. So ingrained in our thinking today it is no longer considered a theory but a fact. Thankfully there are many Creation Scientists who are helping to stem the tide of this deception: however, the vast majority of Christians have been taught evolution throughout their years in public school, and have placed their faith in Darwin and thus rejected Scripture.

What does this have to do with family planning? Evolution is a rival religion to Christianity. Evolution would have you place your faith in a theory about how the world began apart from a Designer. The Bible compels us to place our faith in the One who was there and told us how He made everything. The two cannot be meshed together without severe compromise to His Word. So, if our faith is not in God's Word and His account of Creation, why should we believe Scripture when it talks of children as blessings? If we cannot trust what the Bible says in Genesis chapter 1, why believe what it says in any part of Genesis? Why believe what it says in John 3:16??

We have lost reverence for God's Word as being inerrant (without error). Evolutionary thinking has resulted in us mythologizing the first 11 chapters of Genesis, and thereby not taking God at His word. The natural progression of this way of thinking is that we can somehow marginalize or even disregard God's Word when it suits our own theories, including those of child bearing. This includes making God's Word applicable to only the cultures at those specific times, and therefore not for us today. Having placed Scripture in the realm of fiction, why should we let God plan our families? He can't be trusted in what He's written so why should He be trusted with our reproduction? This is a real likelihood when we do not uphold the Bible as perfect.

Evolution will also lead us to believe that humans are just more highly evolved animals. Millions of years ago we were just part of the lifeless cosmic soup on a newly evolved planet, and look at us today! With the same beginning as all other forms of life, we deny what God has stated in Genesis 1: 25 and 26;

26 *And God said, Let us make man in our image,* **after our likeness: and let them have dominion over the fish of the sea, and over the fowl of the air, and over the cattle, and over all the earth, and over every creeping thing that creepeth upon the earth.**
27 So God created man in his own image, in the image of God created he him; male and female created he them.

God claims He made us in His image. Evolutionists say that this is mythology at best and a lie at worst. In any event, evolutionists are determined that we look at ourselves as having evolved from apes. As animals then, where is the sanctity of life that God claims?

We are unique, not due to accelerated evolutionary processes, but because we are made in His likeness. But if we are indeed animals, why would we think that God has a special plan for us? Why would children be a blessing, rather than just a natural outcome of the sexual union between a male and female? If we have evolved our thinking to the extent that we can control our reproduction and no longer act according to instinct, good for us. Instead of having to swing from tree to tree and forage for food for all our offspring, we can now wear suits and go to the grocery store to feed our 1.6 children per family. We have lost our knowledge that we are "made in the image of God", and now are concerned only with our own self-image.

At roughly the same time that evolution was flooding the minds of our culture, psychology was the next new "science" to solve all of our "problems with living". Dr. Freud, Yung, Maslow, Rodgers, Spock, et al, had the answers we thought we needed. All these men, who founded psychology as we know it today, hated God. They desired a way to explain man's poor behaviour apart from sin. But over the century this line of thinking was just what man wanted to soothe his conscience and convince himself that in all things we are victims, and not to blame for our behaviour.

The church once again failed to stand guard at the gates, and today the Western church is the largest referral service to professional counselling. What this means is that we have lost confidence in God's Word as being sufficient and authoritative. Today we demand people with a long list of credentials, hopefully in psychology, before we can place any trust in what advice they may give us. We look for these same qualifications even in the selection of our Pastors.

What has happened to Christians coming along-side one another in times of need to encourage and correct each other? For the first 1900 years of God's established church there was no such thing as psychology. Did the Holy Spirit forget to put it into the Bible, or did He leave us with an inadequate manual for life? I think it far more likely that we have forgotten that Scripture claims to be sufficient and authoritative.

2 Peter 1

[3] According as his divine power hath given unto us *all* things that pertain unto life and godliness, through the knowledge of him that hath called us to glory and virtue:
[4] Whereby are given unto us exceeding great and precious promises: that by these ye might be partakers of the divine nature, having escaped the corruption that is in the world through lust.
[5] And beside this, giving all diligence, add to your faith virtue; and to virtue knowledge;
[6] And to knowledge temperance; and to temperance patience; and to patience godliness;
[7] And to godliness brotherly kindness; and to brotherly kindness charity.

⁸ For if these things be in you, and abound, they make you that ye shall neither be barren nor unfruitful in the knowledge of our Lord Jesus Christ.
⁹ But he that lacketh these things is blind, and cannot see afar off, and hath forgotten that he was purged from his old sins.

2 Timothy 3
¹⁶ *All* scripture is given by inspiration of God, and is profitable for doctrine, for reproof, for correction, for instruction in righteousness:
¹⁷ That the man of God may be perfect, thoroughly furnished unto all good works.

God has given to us ALL things pertaining to life and godliness, and ALL Scripture is useful for reproof, correction, and instruction. What else do we truly need? Psychology created its own false reproof, correction, and instruction along with its own elite, including child psychologists. We hang on their every word, read all their books, and conduct ourselves accordingly. So when the family psychologist tells us as couples to wait until we "connect" with each other before we think of having children, we obey. When the marriage counsellor suggests that children should wait until we establish our careers, buy a house, and/ or work out our "issues", we go along with the advice. Child bearing gets pushed back further and further, often until it's too late. Psychologists won't confirm that children are the blessing that God says they are

– at least not until we get our lives in order and can properly handle the new stress of being parents.

As we move further into the 20th Century, we see the birth of modern feminism. It was no longer a desire for women to be feminine, but rather to be the same as men. Slowly the role distinctions between men and women became blurred, and equality now became sameness. Feminism dealt a blow to those young women who wanted to be keepers at home, and strongly suggested that Scripture no longer applied in this new, enlightened era. The idea of a young lady staying at home and raising lots of children slowly became obsolete, if not obscene to many women.

With the evolutionary belief that the sanctity of life was meaningless, and the feminist teaching of women having control of their own destiny, Western culture was primed for Margaret Sanger. Her organization created in the 1920's, Planned Parenthood, has promoted the deaths of millions upon millions of children. Sanger was the natural by-product of the culture of that time. Since women were encouraged to be in full control of themselves (the idea of a husband being the head and the wife in a role of submission now a foreign concept), why not fully in control of the fruit of the womb? God was once again shoved aside as being the creator of life, and now the woman was sovereign in family planning. If an "unwanted" pregnancy occurred, Planned Parenthood (or Planned Barrenhood as referred to by some) was there to assist the woman in obtaining an abortion. You see, human life was no longer sacred because we no longer believed we were created in the image of God, but were rather a product of evolution.

If we leap forward to 1973, we have the infamous Roe vs. Wade decision in the USA, which opened the door to legalized abortion. Since then, it has been estimated that over 40 million children have been intentionally murdered through this process in the USA alone. It grieves my heart to even write these statistics, but I'm sure it grieves the heart of our Father in Heaven infinitely more. Not only do we not allow God to be the planner of our families, but when He does provide fruit for the womb, we kill it.

So, today we are immersed in a culture that denies the inerrancy, sufficiency, and authority of Scripture. We are far more interested in pursuing how the world thinks and what the world does. Our church leaders for the most part have jumped on board in droves to this marriage with the world. The modern seeker-sensitive church has created the erroneous philosophy that the more our churches and our people are like the world around us, the more attractive to the unbeliever we will be. In our loss of distinctiveness from the world, we have lost our relevance. Most unbelievers will look at the 21st Century church and its adherents and say "What's the difference? If their life is the same as mine, what's the attraction?" This is an extreme deviation from the church that Christ established as found in Acts 5: 11-14.

[11] **And *great fear came upon all the church, and upon as many as heard these things.***

¹² And by the hands of the apostles were many signs and wonders wrought among the people; (and they were all with one accord in Solomon's porch.
¹³ And of the rest durst no man join himself to them: but the people magnified them.
¹⁴ And believers were the more added to the Lord, multitudes both of men and women.)

What relevance today does a single-income family with a goodly number of children have to the world around us? In one word, HOPE. We have hope where all else is striving to find some kind of meaning. We have a living, active faith that God can be trusted. That God is faithful to His children. That God will bless those willing to be blessed. We have the hope to share with others that God can be held to His Word. That as He blesses the womb, He provides for the children who He claims to be His. That His desire for a godly union is a godly seed. That there is hope yet for a nuclear family where mom and dad love each other, and the father feels rewarded with a full quiver.

CHAPTER SIX

What the future holds

The greatest hope that we have in the future is in the soon return of our LORD and Savior, Jesus Christ. When He establishes His kingdom on this earth, then all will be restored to perfection. Our hope is rightly placed when it is on Jesus.

Even so, before our LORD returns, He warns that the people of the earth will have fallen prey to many deceptions and will have waned in their faith and trust in Him. The words of our LORD are recorded in Luke 18:8;

⁸ I tell you that he will avenge them speedily. Nevertheless when the Son of man cometh, *shall he find faith on the earth*?

Christ's prophetic words remind us that as the return of the LORD approaches, He will find only a remnant of the faithful. Are we to be part of that remnant? Will we remain true to God's Word, even though all would be against us? As the church becomes increasingly worldly and Scripture continues to be compromised, who will stand firm? Is it too large of a sacrifice to separate ourselves from the world when compared with the sacrifice the LORD made on Calvary.

There is nevertheless hope in our future. Hope that the hearts of believers will be turned back to God's perfect, sufficient, and authoritative Word. There is hope if we can disengage our minds from the pattern of the world and choose to have our minds transformed and renewed.

This transformation of thinking is in reality, a step back into the past. Allowing God sovereignty in our family planning is not a new idea or a 21st Century concept. It is to re-establish our faith and our trust in the living God who is the only rock – there is no other. It is a call that Jeremiah gave to Israel to rediscover their love for the LORD and to be obedient. Jeremiah 6:16 reads;

[16] **Thus saith the LORD, Stand ye in the ways, and see, and *ask for the old paths*, where is the good way, and walk therein, and ye shall find rest for your souls. But they said, We will not walk therein.**

These instructions from the LORD are still true for us today. God desires that we would "ask for the old paths". His Holy Spirit will guide us back to the way that we should walk and He will be our guide. May it be a prayer of our hearts that the LORD will teach us where to find these ancient paths, and that we would be empowered by Him to courageously walk His route.

This Scripture goes on to say that these paths are the good way, and that by following them we will find rest for our souls. Blessed rest in Him. Our culture desperately seeks rest for our souls, and we look to recreation and amusements to try to fill this need in our lives. Ultimately, amusements will only temporarily satisfy the flesh, and our souls will continue to seek the rest that only God can provide. His paths, not the world's, are the good way.

But how can allowing the LORD to use our God-given fertility possibly provide rest for our souls? The world will be quick to tell you that children are the cause of stress, not rest. As we walk back and forth in the middle of the night with a crying baby, we may be tempted to think that rest will only come when we finally get these "baby years" behind us and get on with our lives. Once again, our flesh wants to commandeer our thinking, and the world will be only too happy to reinforce the desire of the carnal nature, but we know that God's rest is supernatural. In the midst of a busy home He can provide rest for the soul that far, far exceeds the rest of the flesh.

The people of Israel responded to Jeremiah, and to God, the same way we have been taught to respond, "We will not walk therein". Just as the nation of Israel was bold in their defiance of the LORD, we are the same. We can read what the LORD has to say about the blessing of the fruit of the womb, we can agree that God claims sovereignty over the womb, and we can even accept that He is faithful and true and will meet all of our needs in this area. But just as readily, we can say to the LORD, "We will not walk therein".

We have a completely depraved perception of who we are in God's eyes due to our sin nature. We think we can weigh the evidence from God's Word, and then decide for ourselves whether or not it is in our best interests to obey. God's instructions in His Word are not suggestions though; they are commands. We do not have it within our grasp as created beings to defy the living God. We can bring no better offering to the LORD apart from our obedience. 1Samuel 15:22 reminds us,

²² And Samuel said, Hath the LORD as great delight in burnt offerings and sacrifices, as in obeying the voice of the LORD? Behold, *to obey is better than sacrifice*, and to hearken than the fat of rams.

Our perception of ourselves, and of our position before the Almighty, has also been warped by our sin nature. Whereas the world would have us believe that we are special and of much value, God's Word says otherwise. We read in Job 25:6;

⁶ How much less man, that is a worm? and the son of man, which is a worm?

Compared to God, we are but a worm. A worm cannot defy its master. Just as the clay cannot say to the potter, "What are you doing with me?" We cannot say to God, "Hands off my reproduction!" We need to be transformed in our thinking by the slaying of our flesh and being alive in Christ. We need to be obedient to God's Word, whether it is popular, accepted, divisive, or otherwise.

Because we have not followed God's ancient paths in the past few generations of Western Culture regarding our fertility, we have started, in essence, to kill ourselves off. Through the lack of children in North America and Europe, we have become a dying breed. Christians have joined with the culture to uphold the right to control the number of children we have, and statistics show no discernable difference between believers and non-believers when it comes to family size.

Recent studies have shown that the birthrate in the Western World is less than 2 children per household (Population Reference Bureau, 2004). It doesn't take a mathematician to extrapolate that figure to clearly show that we are not even replacing our own population. The world rejoices with the news that we have now achieved not only zero population growth, but that our numbers are actually in decline. But is our LORD rejoicing? Is this His plan for His people?

If we were to be generous and say that the average believing household has two children, we could then formulate an equation over the next five generations, assuming that the children would follow the example and teaching of their parents. The simple math is that two children, times five generations, is 2 to the power of 5, for a total of 32. After five generations, a believing family who has passed on their faith in God to the fifth generation would now boast 32 believers. Hardly an army. We would need to question if this would provide enough workers for the LORD's harvest?

In contrast, this same equation used for the family who is blessed with eight children and whose example and teaching is passed along for five generations, the math again is now 8 to the power of 5. The total now is in excess of 32,000! It seems almost unbelievable that from one faithful couple who desire children, and for the LORD to bless them as He sees fit, a mid-size town of believers would be the possible result. Now that's an army! Workers that the LORD can mightily use to evangelize and bring hope to a lost world, and for the harvest that the LORD has prepared for us.

John 4
[35] ... I say unto you, Lift up your eyes, and look on the fields; for they are white already to harvest.

If Christians would trust our LORD to bless the fruit of the womb, we would naturally expect that we would have many more children, and thus many more young lives that could be instructed in the ways of the LORD. At the present rate, Satan will win the war against Christians through attrition – and we are cooperating with him, rather than trying to defeat his lies.

David Barrett compiled a Natural Growth Rate chart in the 2001 World Christian Encyclopedia (p. 4).

His statistics reveal that as of 2001, the natural growth rate for Christians in the USA was 1.36, whereas in comparison the growth rate for Muslims in the USA is 2.13. We can forecast that with the growth rate of Muslims far exceeding that of Christians, that by the end of this century, Muslims will be the majority in the USA. If we cannot see the political change in North America that would entail, we need only to look at other Muslim countries around the world to see how the Christians, who are the minority, are often persecuted.

If this present trend continues, and the hearts of believers are not turned back to God and His Word, only the return of the LORD will save us from the coming calamity. Even so, I believe that Christians can stem the tide, and change what the future holds for Western Christianity. We need to return to the ancient paths that the LORD would lead us on. An adventure awaits us as we step out in faith and seek the rest for our souls that only the LORD can provide.

God alone is worthy of our trust. God alone is faithful. He can and will supply for all our needs, according to His riches in Glory. Praise be to the Merciful Father who holds the future in His hands. We have absolutely nothing to fear, if we rest in His loving arms.

CHAPTER SEVEN

What are we afraid of?

Simply put, we are afraid of children. Lots of children. We have become paralyzed at the thought of numerous children living in our homes, and readily entertain doubts that we would be able to handle a house full of kids. We can just as easily believe that those few families who do have several children are "Super Parents" and possess a power that is not available to the average person.

Picture the home with a dozen or so little children tearing around the house, fighting and yelling. Mom is ready to pull her hair out as she stands in the kitchen preparing a meal that could feed an army. Dad is nowhere to be seen, as he is juggling three jobs trying to make ends meet financially. A frightening scene to be sure!

This scenario is what the world has taught us to envision when we think of the possible results of letting the LORD "bless" us with children. Chaos is the expected result of a full quiver, and if you want to maintain your sanity, you'd better have your plan in place to make sure there isn't a population explosion in your own home.

To put it bluntly, this idea of an unruly hoard is a lie. A lie cleverly designed by the father of all lies. With the marriage of the church to the culture around it, this outright lie has been assimilated as the truth, even by the believer. Movies such as Home Alone, or Cheaper by the Dozen, only reaffirm in the minds of the viewers that a larger family can only result in pandemonium.

We need to look at some of these preconceived notions a little closer to see where they can be shown to be untrue. What we're fearful of concerning many children in our homes doesn't have to exist. The blessings we now fear if we allow the LORD to give us children at His pleasure, can be the same blessings greatly sought after if seen in the proper light.

I think we would all agree that by our own observations we know that our LORD typically brings children into families one at a time. Multiple births do, of course, occur on occasion, however in the big picture, these are rare. The scenario I created at the start of this chapter of twelve children (all seemingly to be 5 years of age and under), running wild through the home is what the Devil would like to frighten us with. If the LORD actually blessed you with 12 children, they would in all likelihood be spread over at least 15+ years.

With proper training and guidance, older children in the family can be of great assistance in the functioning of the home. Scripture will instruct the parents how to encourage and discipline children so they may be helpers at home. Young girls and boys can be trained in a variety of chores. The older ones can be paired with the younger ones to ensure that as you head out the door and into the car, that each child is properly dressed, and then buckled into their car-seats. An atmosphere of sharing and caring for each other can become the norm, rather than the exception which is displayed only when guests come for a visit. For further insight on this topic, I would recommend a reading of "To Train Up A Child" by Michael and Debi Pearl.

Well-disciplined and well-behaved children are not only a blessing to the parents, but to everyone else that you come in contact with. As children are trained with proper manners and conduct, they become a wonderful testimony to our LORD. The larger family who has obedient and well-mannered children will often bring out comments of praise from friends and strangers alike. Each one of these comments will enable the parents to give God all the glory for His grace and mercy in your family life.

The idea presented earlier about the absent Dad, having to work three jobs to pay all the bills, is once again reflective only of our having fallen in love with the world and all its entrapments. If we feel that it is a necessity to provide satellite television for our homes, two new vehicles (and their accompanying payments) for our driving pleasure, unlimited sports activities and club programs, exotic vacations, etc., etc., then one income will certainly, in most cases, be inadequate. These "things" are not our needs, however, but our wants.

If it is our heart's desire to meet the needs of our family, and to do away with the lusts of the flesh, then one income will likely suffice. By careful and proper stewardship, and by avoiding the temptation to spend beyond our means, we can avoid becoming ensnared by a debt-load, which can make us feel that it is almost impossible to financially meet the needs of our families. Wonderfully, we can be certain that our LORD is aware of the financial needs of each family, and no matter how unique any given situation may be, the LORD is able to deliver each family from any financial trap we may have fallen, or have been pushed, into. The LORD who owns "the cattle upon a thousand hills" (Ps 50:10) is more than able to meet all our needs.

Families in North America today desperately need the fathers to be present in the home. It is not the LORD's design for the woman to carry on the functions of both the mother and the father. We all know the alarming statistics about absentee fathers, and how many young children are growing up with just a dedicated and devoted mother. But all too often, fathers can be physically present in a home, and yet still be a non-factor in the raising of godly children. Many men have never outgrown their youthful desire for amusements and entertainment, and spend as many hours in front of a television or at sporting events, as they do at a paid job. Their families are given only scraps of their time, and these men eventually grow to even resent that little bit of time when they must be at home.

The Scriptures have many instructions for fathers on their involvement with their children. The LORD will ask each father as he stands before Him in judgment to give an account for how he trained his children, and no excuse will be acceptable to Him. Fathers are reminded of their responsibilities in Psalm 78:5 and again in Ephesians 6:4;

Psalm 78
⁵ For he established a testimony in Jacob, and appointed a law in Israel, which he commanded our *fathers*, that they should make them known to their children:

Ephesians 6
⁴ And, ye *fathers*, provoke not your children to wrath: but bring them up in the nurture and admonition of the Lord.

Having considered the lie that a large family equals chaos, we need to be fully cognizant that by allowing God to be sovereign with our reproduction by no means guarantees that it will result in numerous children. Most of us probably are aware of couples who have been desirous of having children for years, and yet they remain childless. Many couples have a medical condition that preclude them becoming pregnant, or carrying a pregnancy to full-term. Yet again others have spent countless thousands of dollars to try and conceive, often with disappointing results.

For a challenging take on this entire area of in vitro fertilization, I would recommend, "Does God Need Our Help", by John Kilner and C. Ben Mitchell.

Many couples who have given the lordship of their fertility to God have been blessed perhaps only once or twice. Their desire is to welcome as many children as the LORD would provide into their homes, and they are content with what the LORD has blessed them with. I believe that our God is pleased with their heart of obedience in this area of their lives, and they will find subsequent blessings in many areas of their lives. Others have chosen the route of adoption, sometimes of entire families, in order to bring a special blessing to children who are without the love and support of parents.

I am not advocating that we can ascertain the degree to which God has blessed a family by simply counting the number of children they have been blessed with. God's sovereignty is the issue by allowing His will to be done in our lives and allowing Him to bless us as He sees fit. Remember the Master and the talents? He decides how many "talents" to bless us with and we simply receive His blessings and act as His good stewards. We know that the LORD works in each believer's life in different ways, and our desire as His child is to be willing to follow Him wherever He may lead.

Only God knows the hearts of the individuals involved, and we must be careful not to judge others in this matter.

Psalm 139:23
**²³Search me, O God, and know my heart:
try me, and know my thoughts:**

What are the thoughts hidden in our hearts? Are we afraid of what is in store for us should we allow the LORD to control our family planning? We cannot hide anything from the searching of the LORD. If it is in our hearts to disobey God in any manner of living, He will know of it immediately. However, if it is the secret of our heart that we have counted the costs and we are willing to do whatever His good pleasure should be, God will be the rewarder of that faithful person.

What exactly are we afraid of? No doubt we will generate much opposition by allowing God's control over the womb. Most will not understand nor approve, and the lies that the world has created will be thrown in our faces, both by friends and enemies. Despite this, our desire must be to please Him above all else. We must get our eyes off of those around us, and place them squarely on the LORD. He will be our strength and our ever present help in time of troubles. We need not be afraid of anything, but with the LORD's help, we can give Him praise and thanksgiving in all situations.

A brief note here is needed to acknowledge that there are situations in which a pregnancy may cause significant medical risks to the mother, the child, or both. We must realize that what many would classify as a substantial risk to our health is in reality minimal. We should take it upon ourselves to research all information that is given to us concerning medical dangers and determine if there may be a treatment that would eliminate the risks if pregnancy occurred. Nevertheless, there are legitimate concerns in some situations, and as Christians we need to come before the LORD to seek His guidance. He will lead us through these valleys and comfort our souls. Living in a world distorted by sin where all of Creation groans to be restored to its perfect state, we know that our bodies no longer function the way they were designed. But the Designer Himself knows all these things, and He will surely come along side us when our hearts are open to His leading.

2 Timothy 1
[7] For God hath not given us the spirit of fear; but of power, and of love, and of a sound mind.

God has not given us a spirit of fear. If we fear God's sovereignty in our lives, it is a fear of the flesh. The LORD has given into our spirits at the time of our regeneration, power and love and a sound mind. Let us use this power to obey God regardless of any opposition from within or from without. Let us rely on love to increase more and more as we trust our Saviour, and as new and precious lives may be added to our family. And let us use the soundness of our minds to agree with God that He is our all in all, and we are His to do with as He desires. There can be no more logical thing to do than to trust in the One who is faithful and true forever.

CHAPTER EIGHT

Eternal Perspective

A question that has been asked throughout the ages is "What can we take with us to heaven?" Certainly we can understand that we are unable to take with us anything material that we may have accumulated in our lives. This question reminds me of the joke about the rich man being buried in a suit of pure gold so that he would be able to take his wealth to heaven with him. When he arrived in heaven, the angels marveled to each other that someone would come wearing a suit of pavement.

The Scriptures remind us that we are not to hold dear to us any "stuff" while here on earth, as it is all temporal and fleeting. We find in Philippians 3:20 and 1Corinthians 7:31 these reminders from God's Word.

Philippians 3
²⁰ For our conversation is in heaven; from whence also we look for the Saviour, the Lord Jesus Christ:

"Our conversation is in heaven" is translated in the NIV as "our citizenship is in heaven." Heaven is where the believer belongs; it is the home where he longs to be. We make a mistake when we hold onto this life like it's all there is. We need to "look for the Saviour" and keep our focus on Christ. When we consider family planning in light of this Scripture, we need not live in conformity to the world around us. We may live in the USA or Canada, or wherever, but our spiritual birth certificate indicates we are citizens of the kingdom of God. With God as our King, we need to heed His counsel and His guidance without looking around us at what the world is doing.

1 Corinthians 7
³¹ And they that use this world, as not abusing it: for the fashion of this world passeth away.

This world will pass away, and all that is in it. The LORD promises us a new heaven and a new earth at the end of this age. We, however, being made in the image of God, are eternal beings. When we are born into this world, we are born into eternity. Our spirits will never die. Accordingly, there is a choice we need to make while here on the earth, and the result is either eternity in heaven, or eternity in hell. There are no other destinations.

There is a saying that there has never been a person, who while lying on their death bed, has regretted not spending more time at the office. The regret that many people feel, especially later in life, is that they did not invest more of themselves, and more of their time, in relationship building. The relationships on earth that we can most thoroughly pursue are those with our own families. Our spouse should be our best friend as we devote ourselves to honouring and serving them. The ties with our children can be ones of honour and respect for our entire lifetime.

But this leads us to the question of whether or not our relationships that we have enjoyed here on earth continue on into the next life? In a relationship where one is a believer and the other is not, we can say with certainty that the friendship and love they may have had is ended for eternity. The Scriptures are clear that there no longer exists a point of contact between those with Christ in eternity, and those who died apart from their Saviour. Luke 16 is the story of the rich man and Lazarus, and verse 26 specifically tells us;

[26] And beside all this, between us and you there is a great gulf fixed: so that they which would pass from hence to you cannot; neither can they pass to us, that would come from thence.

On the other hand, if both parties in this relationship are believers, we need to consider what Scripture may teach us about knowing one another in heaven. From 2Samuel 12:23 we read of the story of David's infant son who died as a result of David's sin with Bathsheba. After a time of grieving, David declared;

²³ But now he is dead, wherefore should I fast? can I bring him back again? I shall go to him, but he shall not return to me.

David made the assumption that he would be able to both see and recognize his son in heaven, despite the fact that his son died as an infant. Scripture states that when we arrive in heaven, we will "be like Him; for we shall see Him as He is." (1John 3:2). Our earthly bodies were from Adam (1Cor 15:47a), however our resurrection bodies will be like Christ's (1Cor 15:47b). Many people recognized Jesus after His resurrection, so if our LORD was recognizable in His resurrection body, I believe that ours will be the same.

While we remain here on earth let us not forget the wonderful and awesome privilege we have of raising our sons and daughters to be followers of Jesus Christ. If we are faithful in this task, and our children choose Christ, we will then all belong to the family of God. Hence, our children are not only our offspring, but also our brothers and sisters in Christ. Who wouldn't want more of these eternal relationships? As the LORD blesses us with children to nurture in this present life, these special and unique relation-ships can continue in heaven. With the removal of the stain of sin in heaven, how much more beautiful will these relationships be. Our sin now inhibits our true expressions of love, but in heaven there will be no inhibitions. How wonderful to think of carrying on the relationship with our children forever.

When considering an eternal perspective in regard to God's sovereignty in our family planning, we should look at the brevity of this physical life when compared with all of eternity. Several passages of Scripture can be used to remind us that we should not hold on tightly to this life, and that we should be looking to our citizenship in heaven.

James 4
¹⁴ Whereas ye know not what shall be on the morrow. For what is your life? It is even a *vapour*, that appeareth for a little time, and then vanisheth away.

Job 7
⁷ O remember that my life is *wind*: mine eye shall no more see good.

Psalm 39
⁵ Behold, thou hast made my days as an *handbreadth*; and mine age is as nothing before thee: verily every man at his best state is altogether vanity. Selah.

The LORD in His Word describes our lives on this earth as a vanishing vapour, wind, and a handbreadth. With this eternal perspective in mind, let us look afresh at the blessing of children. If we compare the temporal value of careers and cars, houses, sports and vacations, etc., with the eternal perspective of having a perfect relationship forever in the garden of God with those we loved most here on earth, the choice is clear.

How closely we guard not only our possessions, but our very life. Many go to any extreme trying to prolong their life, usually because they are fearful of what happens after they die, and because they have no assurance of salvation. Others want to try to squeeze every imaginable pleasure out of life and end up with nothing but emptiness.

We need to realize that to get the fullest out of this life we need to be obedient to God's commands. Children can be a large part of this fulfillment as we recognize them to be gifts to us by the very hand of God. What utter foolishness to wrap ourselves up in the temporal things in this world and miss out on what the LORD would have for us.

If we could truly have the eternal perspective on our life that the Scriptures declare, we would realize that during this very brief span of time we walk this earth, having many children should be no obstacle whatsoever in finding everlasting joy. If we need to sacrifice a second income, put aside some of our indulgences, and tighten our belts a little, what of it? We may lose out on some of the stuff of the world, but we will gain eternal relationships if we raise our children to love our LORD.

It is a poor trade indeed to exchange God's blessings for what the world calls blessings. We have been convinced that what the world values is of greater worth than what God values – children. Let us walk in His truth, and reject the lie of Satan that many children are part of the curse on mankind.

Eternity is forever. Our lives are but a vanishing mist, and yet we cling to them as if we will live forever in our present condition. But praise the LORD that these bodies are perishing, and we have a glorified body waiting for us. Furthermore, the relationships believing parents can have with their children need not perish. Let us stop thinking of what we may have to give up if the LORD was to bless us with many children, and instead keep our eyes on what joy we can gain through relationships with our children that will never end.

CHAPTER NINE

My testimony regarding my own family

I was raised as the youngest of three children in a liberal Christian home. There was no event, no teaching, nothing whatsoever to cause me to consider early in my life, or to be predisposed to, any of these things I have written about concerning the sovereignty of God in family planning.

After completing four years of University and obtaining a Bachelor of Commerce I was brimming with confidence as I headed out to tackle the world of business. During these four years of schooling, the one truly lasting and valuable thing that occurred was meeting my wife, Michelle. We were engaged soon after I completed schooling, and as I waded into business life, it became clear to me that something was lacking. The missing part of my life was a vibrant relationship with Christ. After a time of self-examination, I confessed to God my sin of failing to acknowledge Him as my LORD. I recall the admission that I had sought to pursue my own path in what career I would undertake, and then asked Him what He would have me do. Well, the LORD answered me clearly, and since that time I have been a front-line police officer – a career spanning some twenty years to date.

Michelle and I were married in 1985, and like most couples, we used birth control to ensure that we weren't going to be surprised with children. After all, we had the master plan for our lives, rather than the Master's plan. It began to unfold according to the blueprint we had designed for our lives, and in 1988 we celebrated the birth of our first son, Joel. He was excitedly received by every one of our relatives, as he was the first grandchild on both sides of the family.

Twenty-one months later, our second son, Jesse, arrived more or less on schedule. Two beautiful boys! Admittedly, there were huge demands on my wife and myself that sapped the energy from our lives. Seeing my wife especially struggle under the demands of two small children, I remember saying to myself, "Two's enough!" After all, I had my wife's best interests in mind, didn't I?

My wife and I continued to use birth control until "somehow" we got pregnant again. Our first daughter, Rachel, was born in 1993. Finally, a girl! Our families and friends quickly forgave us our indiscretion at having a third child now that we had our little girl. So, now we had achieved the perfect family – at least according to our way of thinking.

While Michelle was still breastfeeding Rachel, and prior to any restart of her menstrual cycle, she had the audacity to get pregnant yet again. Eighteen months after Rachel, we were blessed with our second daughter, Naomi. Who could have planned it better? Two boys and two girls. Perhaps a couple more children than what is usually considered acceptable, but not bad, not bad at all.

During this time of our lives, my wife began the task of homeschooling our eldest son. I was dragged reluctantly into this movement, but now find that I am one of its biggest proponents. What an absolute blessing the education of our own children has been to the growth of our family.

Well, time to see the family doctor about "options" – permanent, sterility options. Playing the part of the man, it was decided that I would undergo whatever procedure may be necessary to finally gain control over our fertility. However, and this is the big however, our gracious and merciful Father in heaven was just about to shed His light onto the situation. We had been acting out with the best of our own understanding, but praise Him for His timely intervention.

I clearly recall being in our van on the way to the doctor's for our "talk", when the LORD spoke into my heart and in essence asked me, "What are you doing?" Oh, the flood of emotions. Of course my wife and my four young children had to be in the van with me, taking the opportunity to look every part our LORD's cherubs.

So, good question. What was I thinking? I had no sinister motives in this plan. All things considered, I was doing the right thing, wasn't I? I'm convinced that this is the thinking that many sincere believers are going through at this time of decision. Seeing the pressures of home life, the demands on our time and financial resources it can seem so overwhelming. What happens at this junction is that we lose all perspective on the future.

Believe it or not, things have a way of changing over time. Children actually do grow up, leave the diaper stage behind, and get older. Given enough time, and with proper Biblical training, children can be huge contributors to the functioning of a household. Somehow, in His mercy, God had given me enough of a glimpse of this future as I drove in the van. I never did talk to my doctor about "options".

But, now what? Was it really possible to wean ourselves from the birth control culture? Was my wife going to think I'd gone crazy, or would she receive the same direction from our LORD? Could we take God at His Word that He would meet all our needs? Did we even know what God had to say about this whole issue of family planning?

Again the LORD showed Himself to be the Father of all mercies, and unbeknownst to me, He had been speaking quietly to my wife as well. It grieves me to admit that during this period of searching for God's truths on this issue, it soon became evident that God's people were the most opposed to His sovereignty being exercised in reproduction. In retrospect, I have come to believe that it may be a sense of conviction on the believer's heart that they either never consulted God about this decision, or else over-ruled

Him. Many people we know have had outright angry confrontations about this whole matter with their pastors and/or church leaders. It became apparent that God's Word and His Holy Spirit would be our Counselor.

I remember discussing this issue with one of my former pastors, and his reply was that God had led him to believe that to be effective in his ministry, he would have to limit the number of children in his family at three – hence his subsequent sterilization. I immediately thought of other great evangelical leaders and wondered why the LORD had never revealed this idea to them (eg. Jonathan Edwards had 11 children; A.W. Tozer had 7 children; Martin Luther was blessed with 6 children). I further recall thinking that if the LORD truly wanted him to have just three children, why would the pastor need to get himself sterilized? Wasn't our God able to close the womb of his wife? Does the LORD need surgeons to ensure that reproduction is permanently halted?

In the years that followed, God continued to confirm the truth of His desire to control our reproduction through His Word. My wife and I stepped out in faith, trusting in the everlasting arms of our Savior to meet our every need. Our minds have been transformed (Romans 12:1,2), and we now believe we know what God's perfect will is for our lives in regard to our fertility.

Our journey has taken us from "allowing" the LORD to be sovereign in our family planning, to now greatly desiring Him to bless us with children. Each and every day brings us to the throne of grace where we acknowledge our complete dependency on Him to sustain us. That alone has made the journey immeasurable in worth. Coming before our risen Savior and being in His presence on behalf of ourselves and our children has been the real blessing.

At the time of the writing of this book Michelle and I have just celebrated the birth of our ninth child. We humbly acknowledge that we are incapable of managing this family on our own efforts. He is the One who has made the journey possible, and He is inviting you on the adventure of a lifetime.

Matthew 19
26 But Jesus beheld them, and said unto them, With men this is impossible; but *with God all things are possible.*

Conclusion

I chose the title of this book to be Family UNplanning to remind us that we are to put the entire issue of our reproduction where it rightly belongs – in the hands of our LORD. Family UNplanning may cause us to consider removing from our thoughts and minds a notion that never belonged there in the first place.

Family planning throughout the course of history has rightly fallen under the sovereignty of God. Only in this last century has our culture attempted to rob God of the glory He desires through the raising of godly children. We have succeeded in twisting our thinking of children as being a blessing, a reward and gift from our Heavenly Father to instead viewing them as a curse and a stumbling block to our own fulfillment.

May God in His never-ending grace and mercy forgive us for deliberately limiting our families, and in refusing the blessings that He would give us. Are we so fallen in our natures that we will accept only those blessings from above that help to complete our self-indulgent lifestyle? Will we not diligently seek ALL of what the LORD declares to be blessings directly from the throne room of heaven – including children?

May the LORD give you understanding and wisdom as you seek His will for your lives in regard to family planning. May we magnify and glorify our LORD with lives fully surrendered to Him, for Him to use as He desires.

Genesis 1
[28] And God blessed them, and God said unto them, *Be fruitful, and multiply*, and replenish the earth...

Printed in the United States
91519LV00005B/18/A

9 781600 348518